Jesus
A Story of Love

Written by
Claire Dumont
and Suzanne Lacoursière
Illustrated by
Caroline Merola

Pauline
BOOKS & MEDIA
Boston

Library of Congress Cataloging-in-Publication Data

Dumont, C. (Claire), 1950-
[Jesus. English]
Jesus : a story of love / written by Claire Dumont and Suzanne Lacoursière ; illustrated by Caroline Merola.
p. cm.
Summary: Simple text introduces the life of Jesus and the values and attitudes he taught, such as love, respect, self-giving, prayer, and reconciliation.
ISBN 0-8198-3977-9 (pbk.)
1. Jesus Christ—Biography—Juvenile literature. [1. Jesus Christ—Biography.] I. Lacoursière, Suzanne. II. Merola, Caroline, ill. III. Title.
BT302 .D8413 2003
232.9'01—dc21

2003004335

Original French title: Jesus: une histoire d'amour

Printed and published in the U.S.A. by Pauline Books & Media, 50 Saint Pauls Avenue, Boston, MA 02130-3491.

www.pauline.org

Pauline Books & Media is the publishing house of the Daughters of St. Paul, an international congregation of women religious serving the Church with the communications media.

1 2 3 4 5 6 08 07 06 05 04 03

To all the children of the world, with great love.

This book tells the wonderful story of the life of Jesus. We learned about Jesus when we were children. Little by little he became our best Friend. We love Jesus very much. And we know that he loves us very much. We have written this book to tell you about Jesus. We want you to know him and love him. We're sure that Jesus will become your best Friend, too!

Claire and Suzanne

Long ago, Mary and Joseph traveled to the town of Bethlehem. Mary was going to have a special baby—God's own Son!

Many people were visiting Bethlehem. Mary and Joseph couldn't find a place to sleep. They were tired. They were hungry. Finally, they found a cave to sleep in.

That night, Jesus, the Son of God, was born. It was the first Christmas!

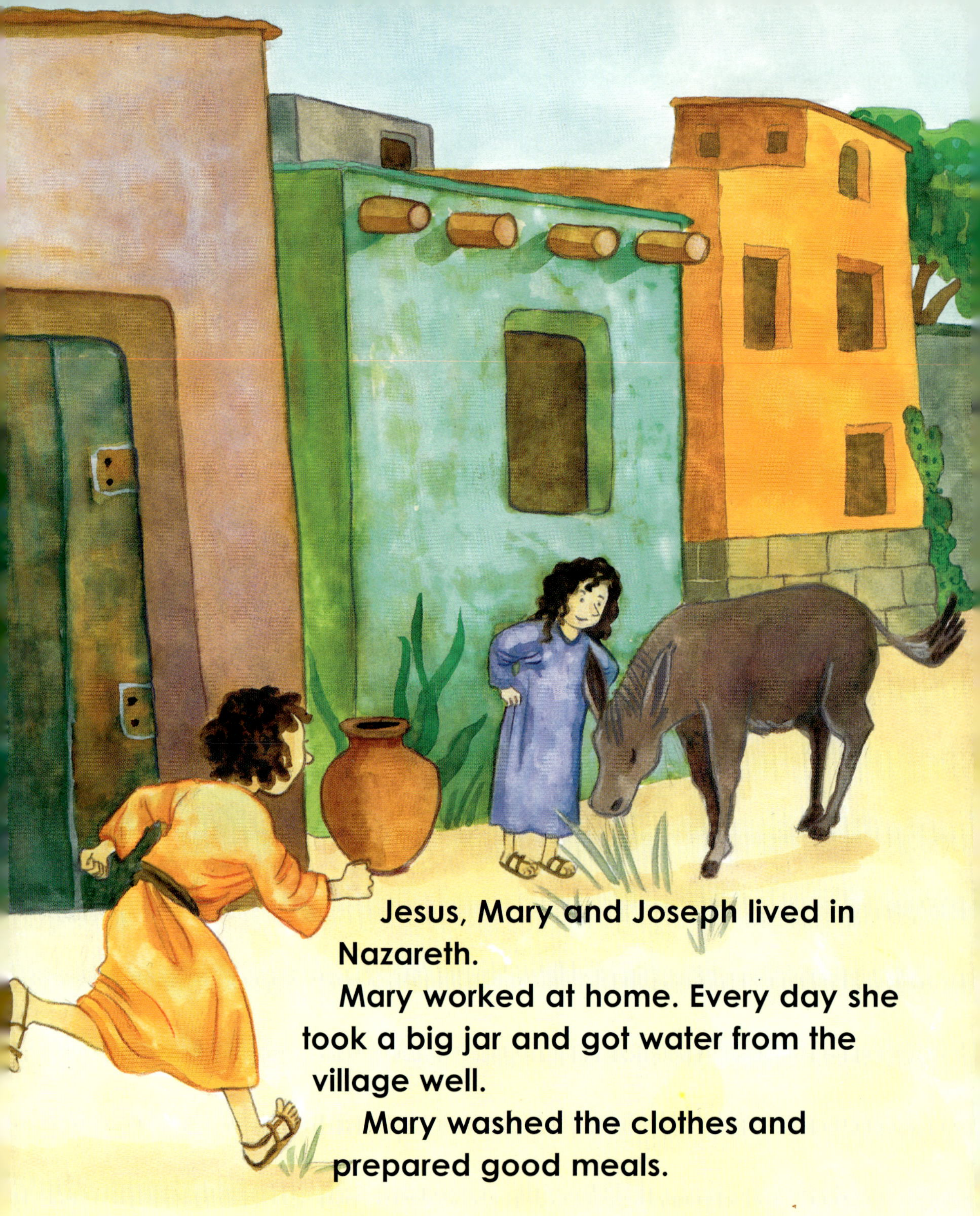

Jesus, Mary and Joseph lived in Nazareth.

Mary worked at home. Every day she took a big jar and got water from the village well.

Mary washed the clothes and prepared good meals.

She kept the house very
clean for Jesus and Joseph.

Joseph was Jesus' legal father on earth.

Joseph was a carpenter.

He worked hard to earn a living for his family.

Every day, Jesus stopped by the carpenter shop to see Joseph.

Sometimes Jesus helped Joseph with his work.

That is how Jesus learned to be a carpenter, just like Joseph.

Jesus learned to read and write in school.

He liked to listen to stories about his Jewish people. He wanted to hear about the Jewish leaders who had lived long ago.

Jesus listened very carefully to stories about Noah, Abraham, Moses, and King David.

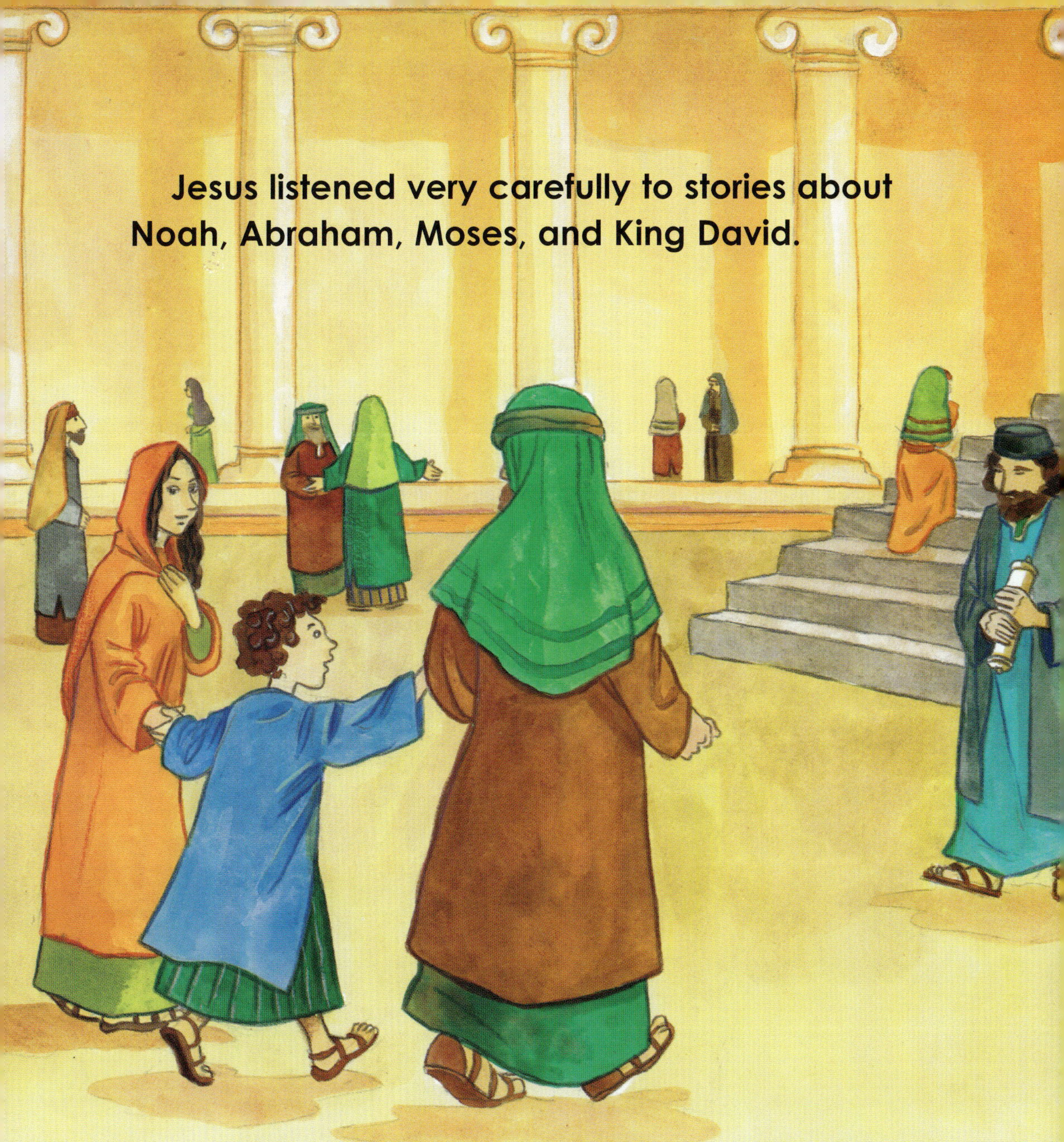

Jesus went to the Temple with Mary and Joseph to pray.

He loved to talk to God his Father. Jesus called God "Abba." "Abba" means "Daddy."

When Jesus grew up he wanted everyone to know about God his Father.

So, Jesus closed the carpenter shop and left Nazareth. He was thirty years old.

Jesus traveled to all the towns and villages of his country. His twelve good friends went with him.

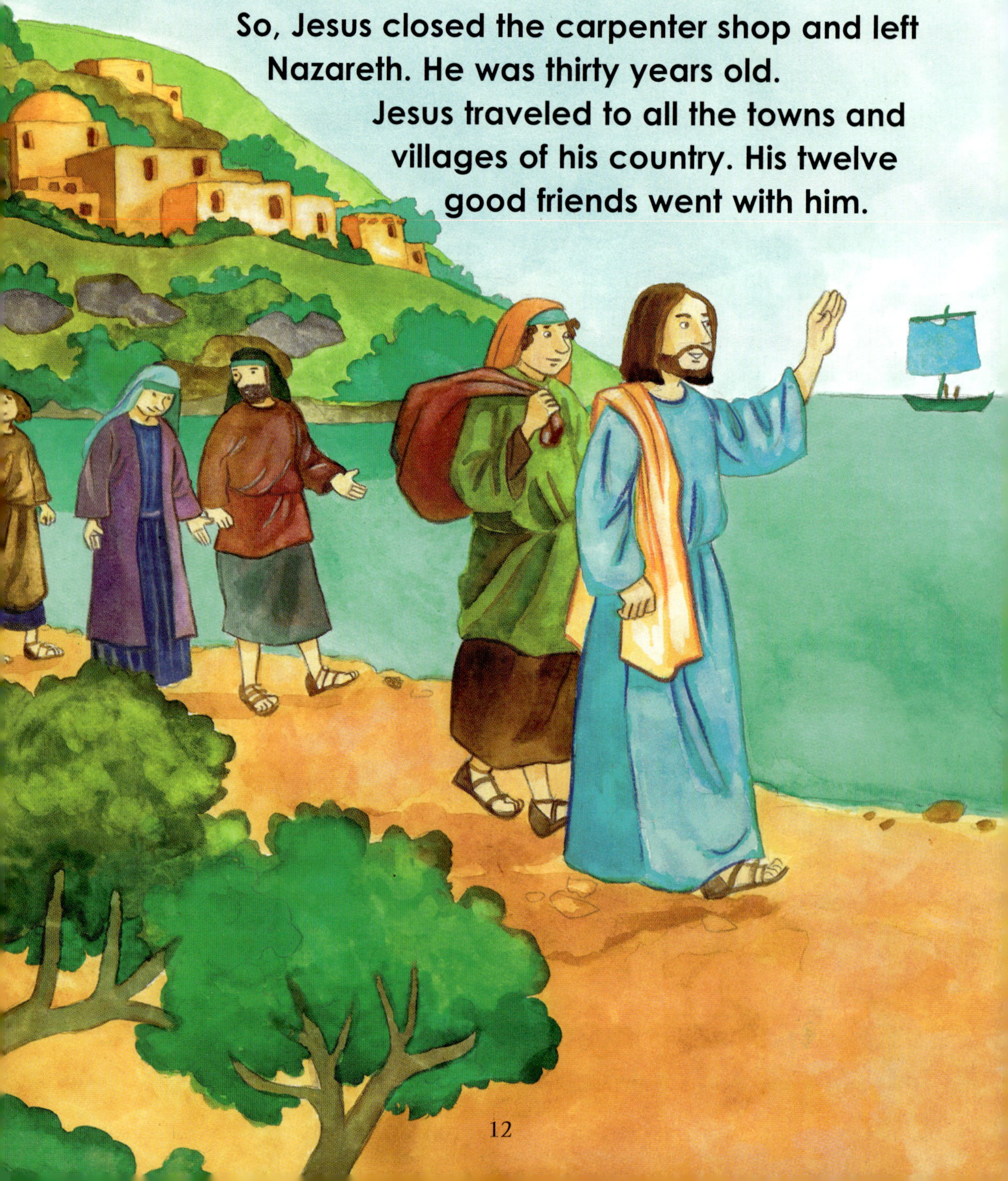

Some days Jesus went fishing with his friends.

He spent most of his time teaching people about God and doing good things to help them. If they were sick, he made them well. If they didn't know what to do, Jesus gave them good advice.

Jesus always talked about love, sharing, and kindness. People liked to listen to his words.

He talked in the villages and cities. He talked to the rich and to the poor. Jesus' words made people's hearts feel happy.

Jesus prayed many times each day to his Father in heaven.

Jesus told people that God loves everyone.

He said that we are all God's children.

One day Jesus' friends said to him: "Teach us to pray!"

So Jesus taught them a prayer.

He said, "This is a prayer to my Father:

"Our Father in heaven,
Your name is holy.
Your kingdom come.
Your will be done on earth
as it is in heaven.
Give us today our daily bread.
Forgive us the wrong things we do
as we forgive those who do wrong things to us.
Do not put us to the test,
but deliver us from evil."

People came from everywhere to see and hear Jesus.

He always welcomed them. He talked with them for a long time.

One day, Jesus did not want to send the people home hungry.

He decided to prepare a big picnic...with the help of his twelve friends.

The people ate the food that Jesus gave them.

After the meal, Jesus told his friends, "Pick up all the leftovers, so nothing will go to waste."

The people went home happy.

Jesus always said:
"Love one another."

Jesus loved
everyone he met.
Jesus took time
to be with people.

He listened to
them carefully.
He was always
ready to help.

Jesus knew that only love can make everyone on earth happy.

Some people didn't like Jesus.

They didn't like some of the things he said.

They didn't like some of the things he did.

They were jealous of Jesus.

One evening Jesus had a special supper with his twelve friends.

Jesus shared a wonderful gift with them. He changed bread and wine into his body and blood.

Jesus asked his friends to love others very much, because love gives life and happiness.

After the meal, Jesus went out to a garden to pray. His friends went with him. Some people who didn't like Jesus sent soldiers to arrest him.

The soldiers put Jesus in jail. The next morning a few men told lies about Jesus.

Then some of the leaders of the people brought him to the governor. They complained about Jesus and asked the governor to punish him. "Jesus, you must die," he said.

Jesus died on the cross because he loves us.

He died to save us from our sins—the wrong things we do.

His Mother was with him. Some of his friends were there, too.

After Jesus died, his friends wrapped his body in a sheet and placed it in a tomb.

God the Father loves Jesus very much.

Jesus is his only Son.

On the third day after he died, Jesus came back to life again!

That day was the first Easter!
Jesus is alive!
He is still with us!

The friends of Jesus soon found out that he was alive.

Some met him in the garden. Others met him in the house where they stayed.

Some friends saw Jesus on the road and near a lake.

Jesus' friends were so happy! They told everyone what they had seen and heard.

We also believe
that Jesus is alive.

We believe that he rose
from the dead.

Even if we can't see Jesus,
we know that he is with us.

Jesus will give us
life...today and always.

Jesus loves us very much!

He wants us to love everyone just as he does.

When we love and are kind, we are like Jesus!

Pauline

BOOKS & MEDIA

The Daughters of St. Paul operate book and media centers at the following addresses. Visit, call or write the one nearest you today, or find us on the World Wide Web, www.pauline.org

CALIFORNIA

3908 Sepulveda Blvd, Culver City, CA 90230 310-397-8676

5945 Balboa Avenue, San Diego, CA 92111 858-565-9181

46 Geary Street, San Francisco, CA 94108 415-781-5180

FLORIDA

145 S.W. 107th Avenue, Miami, FL 33174 305-559-6715

HAWAII

1143 Bishop Street, Honolulu, HI 96813 808-521-2731
Neighbor Islands call: 800-259-8463

ILLINOIS

172 North Michigan Avenue, Chicago, IL 60601 312-346-4228

LOUISIANA

4403 Veterans Memorial Blvd, Metairie, LA 70006 504-887-7631

MASSACHUSETTS

885 Providence Hwy, Dedham, MA 02026 781-326-5385

MISSOURI

9804 Watson Road, St. Louis, MO 63126 314-965-3512

NEW JERSEY

561 U.S. Route 1, Wick Plaza, Edison, NJ 08817 732-572-1200

NEW YORK

150 East 52nd Street, New York, NY 10022 212-754-1110

78 Fort Place, Staten Island, NY 10301 718-447-5071

PENNSYLVANIA

9171-A Roosevelt Blvd, Philadelphia, PA 19114 215-676-9494

SOUTH CAROLINA

243 King Street, Charleston, SC 29401 843-577-0175

TENNESSEE

4811 Poplar Avenue, Memphis, TN 38117 901-761-2987

TEXAS

114 Main Plaza, San Antonio, TX 78205 210-224-8101

VIRGINIA

1025 King Street, Alexandria, VA 22314 703-549-3806

CANADA

3022 Dufferin Street, Toronto, Ontario, Canada M6B 3T5 416-781-9131

1155 Yonge Street, Toronto, Ontario, Canada M4T 1W2 416-934-3440

¡También somos su fuente para libros, videos y música en español!